ANCIENT ROME

ANCIENT CIVILIZATIONS IN REVIEW

By Seth Lynch

Please visit our website, www.enslow.com. For a free color catalog of all our high-quality books, call toll free 1-800-398-2504 or fax 1-877-980-4454.

Library of Congress Cataloging-in-Publication Data
Names: Lynch, Seth, author.
Title: Ancient Rome / Seth Lynch.
Description: Buffalo, New York : Enslow Publishing, 2025. | Series: Ancient
  civilizations in review | Includes index.
Identifiers: LCCN 2024023830 | ISBN 9781978542730 (library binding) | ISBN
  9781978542723 (paperback) | ISBN 9781978542747 (ebook)
Subjects: LCSH: Rome–History–Juvenile literature.
Classification: LCC DG77 .L963 2025 | DDC 937–dc23/eng/20240611
LC record available at https://lccn.loc.gov/2024023830

Published in 2025 by
Enslow Publishing
2544 Clinton Street
Buffalo, NY 14224

Copyright © 2025 Enslow Publishing

Portions of this work were originally authored by Daniel R. Faust and published as *Ancient Rome*. All new material this edition authored by Seth Lynch.

Designer: Leslie Taylor
Editor: Kristen Nelson

Photo credits: Cover (colosseum) Pajor Pawel/Shutterstock.com, (statue) Debbie Ann Powell/Shutterstock.com, (back cover coins) Yaroslaff/Shutterstock.com; Cover and series art (vintage map) Andrey_Kuzmin/Shutterstock.com (brush strokes) ozzichka/Shutterstock.com, (font) MagicPics/Shutterstock.com; p. 5 Peter Hermes Furian/Shutterstock.com; p. 7 Fletcher Fund, 1924/metmuseum.org; p. 9 Palazzo Madama collection/File:Cicero Denounces Catiline in the Roman Senate by Cesare Maccari.png_commons.wikimedia.org; p. 10 Drawing by Silvestre David Mirys/File:Loix des Douze Tables.jpg_commons.wikimedia.org p. 11 Classic Image/Alamy.com; p. 13 Marco Mariani/Shutterstock.com; p. 14 Massimo Todaro/Shutterstock.com; p. 17 Dennis Jarvis (via flickr)/File:Dougga cup-bearers mosaïc.jpg_commons.wikimedia.org; p. 19 Bill Perry/Shutterstock.com; p. 20 lego 19861111/Shutterstock.com; p. 21 PavelJiranek/Shutterstock.com; p. 23 Lucky-photographer/Shutterstock.com; p. 24 Jennifer Nyman/Shutterstock.com; p. 25 (top) Pajor Pawel/Shutterstock.com, (bottom) Sean Pavone/Shutterstock.com; p. 28 stoyanhh/Shutterstock.com; p. 29 (top) AlexAnton/Shutterstock.com, (bottom) Guitar photographer/Shutterstock.com.

All rights reserved. No part of this book may be reproduced in any form without permission in writing from the publisher, except by a reviewer.

Printed in the United States of America

CPSIA compliance information: Batch #CWENS25: For further information, contact Enslow Publishing at 1-800-398-2504.

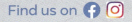

CONTENTS

Founding Rome 4

The Etruscans 6

Roman Republic 8

Taking Over 12

The Time of Caesar 18

The Empire Rises 22

West and East 26

Timeline of Ancient Rome 30

Glossary 31

For More Information 32

Index 32

Words in the glossary appear in **bold** the first time they are used in the text.

Founding Rome

The history of ancient Rome began more than 2,800 years ago around 800 BCE. It started as small villages built near the Tiber River in Italy. Stories say the city of Rome was founded in 753 BCE by brothers named Romulus and Remus.

The word "ancient" means very old or having to do with times long ago.

The Etruscans

Around 600 BCE, a group called the Etruscans **conquered** the city of Rome. Under the Etruscan kings, Rome grew larger and became a powerful city. Then, in 509 BCE, the Romans overthrew the Etruscan king.

The Etruscans **influenced** the art, ideas of life and death, and **literacy** of the ancient Romans.

Etruscan vase

Roman Republic

Rome became a republic. Its main leaders were called consuls. The consuls only served for a year, so they couldn't become too powerful. They worked with members of the Roman **Senate** who could serve for life. The consuls led the Roman armies too.

A republic is a kind of government in which leaders are chosen by the people instead of led by a king or queen. Adult, male Roman **citizens** chose the consuls.

Roman Senate

Two classes made up Roman society. Patricians were the rich, land-owning upper class. Plebeians were the lower class of ordinary, or regular, citizens. For many years of the Roman Republic, plebians didn't have much say in laws or government.

LEARN MORE

Around 450 BCE, Romans started following a set of laws called the Twelve Tables. These laws were written down and posted for all citizens—patrician and plebeian—to read and follow.

writing the Twelve Tables

Taking Over

The Romans soon began to conquer their neighbors. Rome had a powerful, ordered army that was very well trained. With this fighting force, the Romans gained control of the whole Italian **peninsula** by the 270s BCE.

LEARN MORE

Beginning in 312 BCE, the Romans built more than 50,000 miles (80,467 km) of road. These roads joined all of Rome and helped its army move around more easily.

Roman road

Rome fought many wars to become the most powerful **civilization** around the Mediterranean Sea. It fought the empire of Carthage between 264 and 146 BCE in the Punic Wars. It fought the kingdom of Macedonia in four wars between 215 and 148 BCE as well.

# LEARN MORE

An empire is land and countries under the control of one ruler or government.

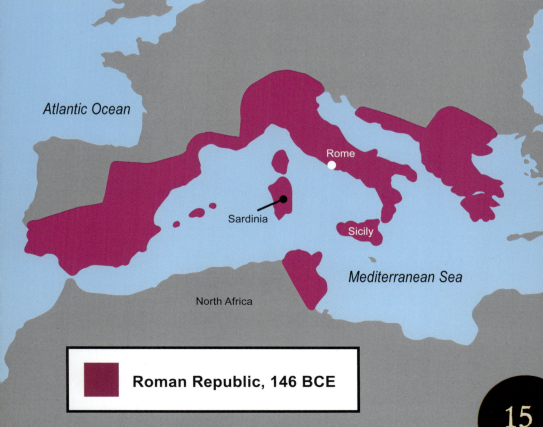

The Roman Republic continued to conquer. The government broke up its large lands into **provinces** to make it easier to govern. However, Roman citizens were unhappy. Life for the rich was much better than that of the common people. This led to war within Rome.

People captured, or taken, from places the Roman Republic conquered were enslaved, or forced to work without pay. Enslaved people often worked for the rich.

The Time of Caesar

Roman general Julius Caesar was elected, or chosen by the people, as a consul of Rome in 59 BCE. In the following years, the army he commanded conquered northwest Europe. However, some members of the Senate thought Caesar was becoming too powerful.

Caesar brought his army to Rome and fought his **rival**, Pompey. Caesar won and named himself dictator of Rome. A dictator was a leader put in place for a short time in times of need.

Julius Caesar

19

Caesar was named dictator of Rome for life in 44 BCE. Not long after, members of the Senate killed Caesar. Caesar's grandnephew Octavian fought those who killed Caesar for power. In 31 BCE, Octavian won and became the leader of Rome.

Roman coin featuring Augustus

LEARN MORE

Octavian became known as Augustus Caesar in 27 BCE when he became the Roman emperor, or ruler.

Augustus Caesar

21

The Empire Rises

The Roman Republic ended when Augustus Caesar became emperor. Under Augustus Caesar and the emperors who followed him, the Roman Empire grew. By 117 CE, it controlled most of Europe, northern Africa, and western Asia. That's about 2 million square miles (5 million km) of land!

As the Roman Empire grew, the Roman culture, or beliefs and ways of life, spread. Roman language, ideas about government, and buildings influenced people around the world.

Augustus Caesar's rule also began almost 200 years of peace in the empire. This time is now called the Pax Romana. Both the Colosseum and the Pantheon were built during this period.

inside the Colosseum

LEARN MORE

Builders finished the Pantheon between 118 and 125 AD. It was a temple, or a building used to honor some of the gods and goddesses the Romans believed in.

Colosseum

Pantheon

West and East

The Roman Empire grew so large that the government couldn't keep control of it all. In 395 CE, the empire was broken into the Western Empire and the Eastern Empire, or the Byzantine Empire. Over time the Byzantine Empire lost much of its Roman culture.

The capital of the Byzantine Empire was Constantinople. The Western Empire's capital was Rome.

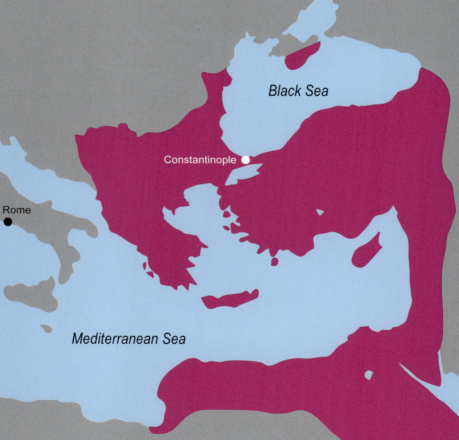

In 410 CE, the city of Rome was destroyed by a group people called the Visigoths. After that, the Western Empire continued to get weaker. It fell in 476 CE. However, parts of the Byzantine Empire continued until the 1400s.

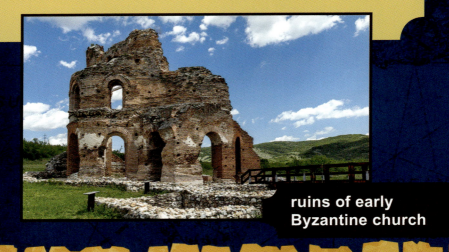

ruins of early Byzantine church

LEARN MORE

The city of Rome gained back some power and is still around today. Constantinople is now the city of Istanbul, Türkiye.

Rome, Italy

Istanbul, Türkiye

Timeline of Ancient Rome

753 BCE .... Stories say Romulus and Remus found Rome.

c. 600 BCE .... The Etruscans conquer Rome.

509 BCE .... Rome becomes a republic.

c. 450 BCE .... The Twelve Tables are written.

312 BCE .... The building of Roman roads begins.

264–146 BCE .... Rome fights wars with Carthage and Macedonia.

59 BCE .... Julius Caesar is chosen as a consul of Rome.

45 BCE .... Julius Caesar defeats Pompey and is first named dictator of Rome.

44 BCE .... Julius Caesar is killed.

31 BCE .... Octavian wins power in Rome.

27 BCE .... Octavian, now Augustus Caesar, is named emperor of the Roman Empire. The Pax Romana begins and lasts for about 200 years.

395 CE .... The Roman Empire breaks into the Western Empire and the Eastern, or Byzantine, Empire.

410 CE .... Rome is destroyed.

476 CE .... The Western Empire falls.

GLOSSARY

citizen: Someone who lives in a country legally and has certain rights.

civilization: Organized society with written records and laws.

conquer: To take by force.

influence: To affect.

literacy: The ability to read and write.

peninsula: A piece of land that is surrounded on three sides by water.

province: An area of a country.

rival: A person who tries to be more successful than another person.

Senate: A governing body in ancient Rome.

society: The people who live together in an organized community with traditions, laws, and values.

FOR MORE INFORMATION

BOOKS

Faust, Daniel R. *The Rise and Fall of Ancient Rome*. Minneapolis, MN: Bearport Publishing Company, 2025.

Simons, Lisa M. Bolt. *Super Surprising Trivia About Ancient Civilizations*. North Mankato, MN: Capstone Press, 2024.

WEBSITE

National Geographic Kids: Ancient Rome Facts and History
https://kids.nationalgeographic.com/history/article/ancient-rome
Read more about ancient Rome here.

Publisher's note to educators and parents: Our editors have carefully reviewed this website to ensure it is suitable for students. Many websites change frequently, however, and we cannot guarantee that a site's future contents will continue to meet our high standards of quality and educational value. Be advised that students should be closely supervised whenever they access the internet.

INDEX

Byzantine Empire, 26, 27, 28, 29
Caesar, Julius, 18, 19, 20, 21
Etruscans, 6, 7
fall of Rome, 28
government, 8, 9, 18, 20, 22, 24, 26
Octavian (Augustus Caesar), 20, 22, 24

Pax Romana, 24
religion, 24
slavery, 16
society, 10, 11
Tiber River, 4
Twelve Tables, 10
war/army, 8, 12, 14, 15, 16, 18, 28